Francis Frith's
WELSH CASTLES

Francis Frith's
WELSH CASTLES

◆

Clive Hardy

First published in the United Kingdom in 2000 by
Frith Book Company Ltd

Hardback Edition 2000
ISBN 1-85937-120-5

Paperback Edition 2001
ISBN 1-85937-322-4

Reprinted in Paperback 2003

British Library Cataloguing in Publication Data

Welsh Castles
Clive Hardy

Frith Book Company Ltd
Frith's Barn, Teffont,
Salisbury, Wiltshire SP3 5QP
Tel: +44 (0) 1722 716 376
Email: info@frithbook.co.uk
www.frithbook.co.uk

Frontcover: **RAGLAN**, *the Castle 1906* 54519

Frontispiece: **CRICCIETH**, *the Castle 1931* 84766

The colour-tinting is for illustrative purposes only, and is not intended to be historically accurate

Printed and bound in Great Britain

CONTENTS

FRANCIS FRITH: *Victorian Pioneer*

FRANCIS FRITH, Victorian founder of the world-famous photographic archive, was a complex and multitudinous man. A devout Quaker and a highly successful Victorian businessman, he was both philosophic by nature and pioneering in outlook.

By 1855 Francis Frith had already established a wholesale grocery business in Liverpool, and sold it for the astonishing sum of £200,000, which is the equivalent today of over £15,000,000. Now a very rich man, he was able to indulge his passion for travel. As a child he had pored over travel books written by early explorers, and his fancy and imagination had been stirred by family holidays to the sublime mountain regions of Wales and Scotland. 'What lands of spirit-stirring and enriching scenes and places!' he had written. He was to return to these scenes of grandeur in later years to 'recapture the thousands of vivid and tender memories', but with a different purpose. Now in his thirties, and captivated by the new science of photography, Frith set out on a series of pioneering journeys to the Nile regions that occupied him from 1856 until 1860.

INTRIGUE AND ADVENTURE

He took with him on his travels a specially-designed wicker carriage that acted as both dark-room and sleeping chamber. These far-flung journeys were packed with intrigue and adventure. In his life story, written when he was sixty-three, Frith tells of being held captive by bandits, and of fighting 'an awful midnight battle to the very point of surrender with a deadly pack of hungry, wild dogs'. Sporting flowing Arab costume, Frith arrived at Akaba by camel seventy years before Lawrence, where he encountered 'desert princes and rival sheikhs, blazing with jewel-hilted swords'.

During these extraordinary adventures he was assiduously exploring the desert regions bordering the Nile and patiently recording the antiquities and peoples with his camera. He was the first photographer to venture beyond the sixth cataract. Africa was still the mysterious 'Dark Continent', and Stanley and Livingstone's historic meeting was a decade into the future. The conditions for picture taking confound belief. He laboured for hours in his wicker dark-room in the sweltering heat of the desert, while the volatile chemicals fizzed dangerously in their trays. Often he was forced to work in remote tombs and caves

where conditions were cooler. Back in London he exhibited his photographs and was 'rapturously cheered' by members of the Royal Society. His reputation as a photographer was made overnight. An eminent modern historian has likened their impact on the population of the time to that on our own generation of the first photographs taken on the surface of the moon.

VENTURE OF A LIFE-TIME

Characteristically, Frith quickly spotted the opportunity to create a new business as a specialist publisher of photographs. He lived in an era of immense and sometimes violent change. For the poor in the early part of Victoria's reign work was a drudge and the hours long, and people had precious little free time to enjoy themselves.

Most had no transport other than a cart or gig at their disposal, and had not travelled far beyond the boundaries of their own town or village. However, by the 1870s, the railways had threaded their way across the country, and Bank Holidays and half-day Saturdays had been made obligatory by Act of Parliament. All of a sudden the ordinary working man and his family were able to enjoy days out and see a little more of the world.

With characteristic business acumen, Francis Frith foresaw that these new tourists would enjoy having souvenirs to commemorate their days out. In 1860 he married Mary Ann Rosling and set out with the intention of photographing every city, town and village in Britain. For the next thirty years he travelled the country by train and by pony and trap, producing fine photographs of seaside resorts and beauty spots that were keenly bought by millions of Victorians. These prints were painstakingly pasted into family albums and pored over during the dark nights of winter, rekindling precious memories of summer excursions.

THE RISE OF FRITH & CO

Frith's studio was soon supplying retail shops all over the country. To meet the demand he gathered about him a small team of photographers, and published the work of independent artist-photographers of the calibre of Roger Fenton and Francis Bedford. In order to gain some understanding of the scale of Frith's business one only has to look at the catalogue issued by Frith & Co in 1886: it runs to some 670

pages, listing not only many thousands of views of the British Isles but also many photographs of most European countries, and China, Japan, the USA and Canada – note the sample page shown above from the hand-written *Frith & Co* ledgers detailing pictures taken. By 1890 Frith had created the greatest specialist photographic publishing company in the world, with over 2,000 outlets – more than the combined number that Boots and WH Smith have today! The picture on the right shows the *Frith & Co* display board at Ingleton in the Yorkshire Dales (left of window). Beautifully constructed with a mahogany frame and gilt inserts, it could display up to a dozen local scenes.

POSTCARD BONANZA

The ever-popular holiday postcard we know today took many years to develop. In 1870 the Post Office issued the first plain cards, with a pre-printed stamp on one face. In 1894 they allowed other publishers' cards to be sent through the mail with an attached adhesive halfpenny stamp. Demand grew rapidly, and in 1895 a new size of postcard was permitted called the

court card, but there was little room for illustration. In 1899, a year after Frith's death, a new card measuring 5.5 x 3.5 inches became the standard format, but it was not until 1902 that the divided back came into being, with address and message on one face and a full-size illustration on the other. *Frith & Co* were in the vanguard of postcard development, and Frith's sons Eustace and Cyril continued their father's monumental task, expanding the number of views offered to the public and recording more and more places in Britain, as the coasts and countryside were opened up to mass travel.

Francis Frith died in 1898 at his villa in Cannes, his great project still growing. The archive he created continued in business for another seventy years. By 1970 it contained over a third of a million pictures of 7,000 cities, towns and villages. The massive photographic record Frith has left to us stands as a living monument to a special and very remarkable man.

Frith's Archive: *A Unique Legacy*

FRANCIS FRITH'S legacy to us today is of immense significance and value, for the magnificent archive of evocative photographs he created provides a unique record of change in 7,000 cities, towns and villages throughout Britain over a century and more. Frith and his fellow studio photographers revisited locations many times down the years to update their views, compiling for us an enthralling and colourful pageant of British life and character.

We tend to think of Frith's sepia views of Britain as nostalgic, for most of us use them to conjure up memories of places in our own lives with which we have family associations. It often makes us forget that to Francis Frith they were records of daily life as it was actually being lived in the cities, towns and villages of his day. The Victorian age was one of great and often bewildering change for ordinary people, and though the pictures evoke an impression of slower times, life was as busy and hectic as it is today.

We are fortunate that Frith was a photographer of the people, dedicated to recording the minutiae of everyday life. For it is this sheer wealth of visual data, the painstaking chronicle of changes in dress, transport, street layouts, buildings, housing, engineering and landscape that captivates us so much today. His remarkable images offer us a powerful link with the past and with the lives of our ancestors.

TODAY'S TECHNOLOGY

Computers have now made it possible for Frith's many thousands of images to be accessed almost instantly. In the Frith archive today, each photograph is carefully 'digitised' then stored on a CD Rom. Frith archivists can locate a single photograph amongst thousands within seconds. Views can be catalogued and sorted under a variety of categories of place and content to the immediate benefit of researchers. Inexpensive reference prints can be created for them at the touch of a mouse button, and a wide range of books and other printed materials assembled and published for a wider, more general readership. The day-to-day workings of the archive are very different from how they were in Francis Frith's

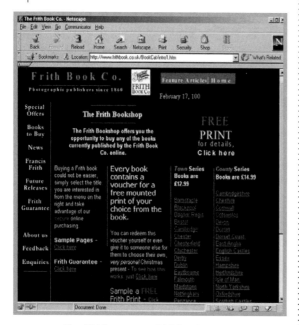

See Frith at www. frithbook.co.uk

time: imagine the herculean task of sorting through eleven tons of glass negatives as Frith had to do to locate a particular sequence of pictures! Yet the archive still prides itself on maintaining the same high standards of excellence laid down by Francis Frith, including the painstaking cataloguing and indexing of every view.

It is curious to reflect on how the internet now allows researchers in America and elsewhere greater instant access to the archive than Frith himself ever enjoyed. Many thousands of individual views can be called up on screen within seconds on one of the Frith internet sites, enabling people living continents away to revisit the streets of their ancestral home town, or view places in Britain where they have enjoyed holidays. Many overseas researchers welcome the chance to view special theme selections, such as transport, sports, costume and ancient monuments.

We are certain that Francis Frith would have heartily approved of these modern developments, for he himself was always working at the very limits of Victorian photographic technology.

THE VALUE OF THE ARCHIVE TODAY

Because of the benefits brought by the computer, Frith's images are increasingly studied by social historians, by researchers into genealogy and ancestory, by architects, town planners, and by teachers and schoolchildren involved in local history projects. In addition, the archive offers every one of us a unique opportunity to examine the places where we and our families have lived

and worked down the years. Immensely successful in Frith's own era, the archive is now, a century and more on, entering a new phase of popularity.

THE PAST IN TUNE WITH THE FUTURE

Historians consider the Francis Frith Collection to be of prime national importance. It is the only archive of its kind remaining in private ownership and has been valued at a million pounds. However, this figure is now rapidly increasing as digital technology enables more and more people around the world to enjoy its benefits.

Francis Frith's archive is now housed in an historic timber barn in the beautiful village of Teffont in Wiltshire. Its founder would not recognize the archive office as it is today. In place of the many thousands of dusty boxes containing glass plate negatives and an all-pervading odour of photographic chemicals, there are now ranks of computer screens. He would be amazed to watch his images travelling round the world at unimaginable speeds through network and internet lines.

The archive's future is both bright and exciting. Francis Frith, with his unshakeable belief in making photographs available to the greatest number of people, would undoubtedly approve of what is being done today with his lifetime's work. His photographs, depicting our shared past, are now bringing pleasure and enlightenment to millions around the world a century and more after his death.

WELSH CASTLES – *An Introduction*

NATIVE WELSH AND NORMAN WARLORD

The earliest castles were built in Normandy. Duke Richard I (942-996) built a stone stronghold at Rouen and fortified a palace at Bayeux. Richard II (996-1026) and Richard III (1026-27) raised castles at Tillieres, Falaise, Le Homme, Cherbourg, and Brix. But it would be under the dukedom of William the Bastard that the relationship between castles, lordship, and control, would manifest itself and be expanded upon. In 1047 William built a castle at Caen, part of an overall strategy that would allow him to exercise political, social and military control over lower Normandy. That same year he defeated rebel Norman lords at Val-les-Dunes and ordered their castles destroyed.

There were a handful of castles in England before the Conquest, built by Norman lords who had settled in the country at the invitation of Edward the Confessor. Such castles are known to have existed at Hereford, Ewyas Harold, and Richard's Castle. Less certain in date are those at Clavering in Essex and Dover Castle. Richard's Castle was a motte and bailey built in Herefordshire prior to 1051 by Richard FitzScrob, and was successfully defended by him against an assault during the anti-Norman rising led by Godwin, Earl of Wessex. Dover might have been a pre-invasion stronghold, as both William of Poitiers and Eadmer the monk-chronicler relate that when Harold swore his now famous oath to William in 1064 he also promised to give him possession of Dover Castle (castrum Doverum). Harold could, however, have been referring to some earlier Anglo-Saxon fortification or to a castle. Either way, the lack of any firm evidence leaves interpretation open to speculation.

William the Conqueror took little active role in the overrunning of Wales; he was more than happy to leave it to men he trusted. In any case, William had more than enough on his hands trying to hold on to England. William's hold on the country was tenuous to say the least; he may have won the Battle of Hastings and been offered the crown, but England was far from his.

Cornwall, Mercia, Kent and the North rose in open revolt; the Northumbrians who had taken no part in the fighting at Hastings were behind two rebellions in 1069. The second of these was by far the most dangerous for William. It was supported by a Danish fleet in the Humber, and the city of York was in Danish hands. However, as William moved northwards the Danes abandoned York and fell back on the Isle of Axholme. If William thought matters would soon be over, he was wrong: the Mercians, aided by the Welsh, also took to the field. Against all the rules of war, William divided his forces. Leaving a force to watch the Danes, he moved with the main body of his army towards Stafford, where he won an easy victory. By the end of the year, William was on the Tees when news of a second Mercian revolt reached him. Crossing the Pennines, William moved into Cheshire, establishing a castle at Chester, and then on to Stafford where another stronghold was erected.

The Conqueror's reprisals during 1069-70 were acts of deliberate cold-blooded savagery so that Celt, Anglo-Saxon, and Dane alike would lose the will to fight and resistance would be crushed once and for all. Almost the whole of the population of north Lancashire was driven out, and over half the villages in the North Riding, and one third in both the East and West Ridings, were laid waste. Symeon of Durham wrote of William's harrying of the North. He described the devastation wrought upon towns, villages and farmsteads, and of corpses left to rot where they had fallen. That William allowed men like William Fitz Osbern, Lord of Breteuil, to undertake the Norman expansion into Wales whilst he looked after England shows that he trusted them in all things. Norman inroads into Wales were slow, possibly deliberately so, as the full weight of the Norman war machine could not be fully committed until the pacification of the English was complete. The Normans were, however, able to take full advantage of the internal dissent that plagued Wales; it was little better than a rag-tag of

MONMOUTH CASTLE 1896 38693   *Built by William Fitz Osbern as part of the Norman expansion into Wales*

petty kingdoms ruled by feuding princes. But we should not forget that the invaders also met with dogged resistance from leaders like Rhys ap Tewdwr, and in 1094 the Welsh inflicted a defeat on the Normans at Coed Yspwys.

The reign of Henry I saw Norman domination spread over much of Wales; the Gower peninsula and Pembrokeshire became so back. Henry agreed to recognise Owain Gwynedd's lands in the north and Rhys' in the south. Native Welsh lords built castles for themselves, though the earliest written evidence for one comes from the 'Brut y Tywysogyon'. In the entry for the year 1111 is a reference to Cadwgan ap Bleddyn being killed at Welshpool where he had 'thought to

PENNARD CASTLE 1893 32760

populated with colonists that the Welsh language all but disappeared from the area. The King's death in 1135 plunged England into civil war and anarchy. The Welsh under Owain Gwynedd rose in rebellion, driving the Normans from much of North Wales. It was the beginning of a period that would see Wales produce several able and determined leaders that included Rhys ap Gruffydd, whose stronghold was at Dynevor Castle. In 1165 Welsh leaders put their differences to one side and combined their forces to defeat Henry II's Anglo-French army. The alliance did not last: Rhys and Owain Gwynedd turned on Owain Cyfeiliog, and Henry was soon stay and make a castle'.

Llywelyn ap Iorwerth became ruler of Gywnedd in 1201. By 1211 his power and influence was such that his own father-in-law, King John, launched an invasion of Wales which was supported of a number of Welsh lords, forcing Llywelyn to come to terms. Llywelyn might have been down, but he certainly wasn't out. In 1215 he actively sided with the barons against John, and in later years further strengthened his position in alliances cemented by the marriages of his daughters Gwladus and Helen into the powerful de Braose and de Blundeville families. The Baron's War weakened John's ability to hold Llywelyn in check. Llywelyn not only secured Welsh rights in Magna Carta, but now attempted to change the social structure of Wales by encouraging the adoption of Norman feudal and manorial systems in place of the tribal loyalties of old. For a few years Wales experienced something close to unity under an able leader; but Llywelyn's death in 1240 created a power vacuum - there was no one of his calibre to take on the task. The eventual successor was Llywelyn ap Gruffydd, grandson of the great man, who would go down in history as the first and only native Prince of Wales. Llywelyn's title was recognised by Henry III, and in return Llywelyn acknowledged Henry as his overlord. The mistake Llywelyn made was not with Henry, but with his successor Edward I. Edward Longshanks would become the most able and most ruthless king ever to sit on the throne of England. The first mistake Llywelyn made was in not attending Longshanks' coronation in 1274. His second was in attacking English border areas in 1277. There could be but one response.

EDWARD LONGSHANKS

In the summer of 1277 Edward was ready to move against Llywelyn ap Gruffydd. His army would attack from three bases, Chester, Montgomery and Carmarthen, with Longshanks himself at the head of the most northern force. On leaving Chester, Edward made for Flint, where he ordered the building of a castle and the establishment of a fortified burgh. From Flint the army made its way to Rhuddlan, already a strategic site with a history of fortification going back five hundred years, and once the stronghold of Gruffydd ap Llywelyn. Here, too, Edward ordered a castle to be built. Construction must have begun almost immediately, as there are surviving accounts dating from 14 September 1277. Rhuddlan was designed by Edward's brilliant engineer-architect Master James of St George. The work progressed quickly, as the fortress was able to withstand a Welsh assault in 1282. Rhuddlan's most famous captive was Dafydd ap Gruffydd, brother of Llywelyn, Prince of Wales, who was held here prior to his being taken to Shrewsbury where he was hung, drawn, and quartered. Edward was at Rhuddlan when the head of Llywelyn was brought to him. The prince had died at the hands of a common soldier near Aberedw Castle; his head was then cut from his body and sent to Longshanks. Afterwards the head was sent to London to be displayed upon a stake outside the Tower. Edward's first war against the Welsh resulted in castles being built at Flint, Rhuddlan, Aberystwyth and Builth, and a number of older ones, including captured Welsh strongholds, being remodelled and refortified.

Edward's campaign of 1282-83 came with an added dimension: not only was he determined to finish off Llywelyn ap Gruffydd once and for all, but he would also stamp his authority upon the Welsh in such a way that they would have little doubt as to who was the ruler and who were the ruled.

The first would be by force of arms, the latter by a programme of castle-building on a scale never before seen in Wales. Throughout the shires of England county sheriffs were instructed to impress workers for service in Wales. Masons, carpenters, diggers and woodcutters were ordered to Chester, where they were assigned to particular projects. Though Chester was the principal assembly point, Bristol was used for the contingents raised in Gloucestershire, Somerset and Dorset. These men were taken by boat to Carmarthen, from whence they were to walk to Aberystwyth. The number of workers raised varied from one county to another. Northumberland sent 10 carpenters and 40 diggers; Lincolnshire raised 40 carpenters, 20 masons and 150 diggers; Wiltshire sent 10 carpenters, 20 diggers and a large number of woodcutters. The other counties to supply woodcutters were Derbyshire, Nottinghamshire, Staffordshire, Shropshire, Herefordshire, Gloucestershire, Warwickshire and Leicestershire.

Much of the work tended to be seasonal, but the gangs of skilled workers were kept together throughout the winter months preparing stone and timber. Such forward planning allowed construction to get under way again as soon as the weather picked up.

Between 1277 and 1304 Longshanks spent an estimated £80,000 on castle building in North Wales. Most of the money went on new construction, though sums were spent on remodelling existing fortresses. The money was raised by taxation: Edward levied nine taxes between 1275 and 1306, which together netted him about £500,000. Caernarvon and its town walls cost £19,900, Beaumaris £14,500, Harlech £8000, Rhuddlan £9000 and Flint £7000. Builth was the smallest of Edward's castles. It was built on the banks of the Upper Wye; construction began in May 1277 on the site of a late 11th-century Norman motte and bailey raised by Philip de Braose. It comprised a circular motte surrounded by a deep ditch and two platform baileys, also surrounded by ditch defences.

RAGLAN CASTLE 1906 54519

Work on Builth ceased during 1282 for lack of funds.

Madoc's revolt of 1294 would result in the building of the last of the Edwardian fortresses. The Welsh overran Anglesey and hanged Roger de Pulesdon, the King's sheriff, friend, and trusted servant. Retribution was swift and brutal, with Longshanks deciding to campaign throughout the winter of 1294-95. In order to keep Anglesey in check, a new fortress was built at Beaumaris. The castle might have been projected as early as 1283, but it was put on hold until Madoc's escapade called for the plans to be dusted off. By the autumn of 1295, over £6000 had been spent on Beaumaris; by the end of February 1296, it was already defendable, with the curtains of the inner ward and the flanking towers of the two gatehouses already standing at least thirty feet high.

THE CIVIL WAR

At the commencement of the First English Civil War, Pembroke was the only castle in Wales to have a Parliamentarian garrison. All the others in a fit enough state to be garrisoned were held in the name of Charles I. The Second Civil War lasted from 5 May 1646 to 30 January 1649; once again, a number of castles were held by the Royalists. Raglan, with its 800-strong garrison, was besieged from May to August 1646, but the Parliamentarians made little progress until Colonel Morgan took over and requested heavy artillery so that both town and castle could be bombarded. On 8 August Sir Thomas Fairfax arrived to take personal command, and immediately offered terms to the Marquess of Worcester. On the 19th the garrison marched out, hav-

ing been accorded the full honours of war: fully armed, banners flying, drums beating. Only the marquess was detained, taken into custody and placed at the mercy of Parliament. Already an old man, he died before being brought to trial. With the fall of Raglan, the only other fortress in Royalist hands was Harlech, which held out until 16 March 1647.

Events took a turn on 23 March 1648, when a dispute over arrears of pay led Colonel Poyer, Governor of Pembroke Castle, to change sides and declare for the King. Pembroke was besieged from 22 May to 11 July by Cromwell himself. With his light artillery making little impact, Cromwell ordered heavy guns to be brought by sea. These arrived on 1 July, and the bombardment of town and castle began ten days later. Terms were offered, and as food and water supplies were critical, they were accepted. The garrison would be allowed to leave and go home; the officers were to leave England; Colonels Poyer, Laughan, and Powell were to be given over to the mercy of Parliament. All three were subsequently tried and sentenced to death. However, the Army Council were feeling lenient and decreed that the three would draw lots. The two who drew pieces of paper upon which were written the words 'Life given by God' would be spared; the one who drew the blank piece of paper would be executed. Colonel Poyer met his end before a firing squad in Covent Garden.

Parliament ordered the slighting of a large number of castles in order to make them militarily untenable. They would be of no use to the Royalists and pose no threat to Parliament. Slighting varied from one castle to another: some were hardly touched, others were almost obliterated. Measures ordered against Welsh castles but not necessarily carried out were: Aberystwyth (blown up); Abergavenny (substantial demolition); Caernarvon (make untenable); Cardigan (extensive demolition); Carmarthen (make untenable); Chirk (Major General Lambert to see castle demolished and made untenable); Conwy (Scottish Committee to consider how garrison may be slighted); Denbigh (extensive demolition); Flint (extensive demolition); Harlech (demolition of outer curtain); Haverfordwest (some demolition); Monmouth (dismantle works); Montgomery (demolish, material to be sold for paying costs); Newcastle Emlyn (negotiations with owner for assurances it will not be used against Parliament); Raglan (extensive demolition, all materials to be sold to best advantage of the State); Powis Castle (outworks to be demolished, walls breached); Rhuddlan (slight new works); Swansea (disgarrison and slight).

When Raglan was slighted, the sale of lead stripped from its roofs brought in £8000. It did, of course, cost money to slight a fortress. On 11 June 1649 the Council of State ordered the complete demolition of Monmouth Castle, though its owner, Richard Lord Herbert of Cherbury was allowed £1611-10s for his losses, which would be deducted from his £4000 fine for supporting the King. The work took four months, and salvaged material was offered for sale. The pay rates for workers were gradually reduced as the weeks went by. Carpenters were on 2s 6d a day at the start, but only on 1s 3d during the last couple of weeks or so. Similarly, the wages of masons dropped from 1s 6d a day to 1s, miners from 2s to 1s 4d, and labourers from 1s to 10d.

RAGLAN CASTLE 1906 54519

ABERGAVENNY CASTLE 1914 67673

This was considered to have been the most important de Braose stronghold after Brecon. In 1172 Abergavenny fell to Sytsylt ap Dyferwald, but was soon restored to its Norman lord. William de Braose, Lord of Brecon, Radnor and Builth, was not a man to be crossed. He invited Sytsylt, his son Geoffrey and a number of their retainers to Abergavenny to celebrate Christmas. They were butchered to a man. The Welshmen were avenged by friends and allies who burnt the castle and captured its garrison.

ABERYSTWYTH CASTLE 1892 30285

Designed by Edward I's brilliant fortifications expert Master James of St George, Aberystwyth was one of a line of coastal fortresses built by Longshanks in order to impose his will upon the Welsh. It remained an important English garrison until 1404, when it fell along with Harlech and Criccieth to Owain Glyndwr. Recaptured by the English in 1407, it fell again to Glyndwr in 1408, but he was only able to hold on to it for a few months before it was once again in English hands.

ABERYSTWYTH CASTLE 1903 50810

The ragged remains of Aberystwyth were transformed into public gardens by the local council and became a popular place for holidaymakers and trippers alike. Here on a sunny afternoon in 1903 the crowd gathers to enjoy the antics of a Pierrot troupe; they are the men in the white silk clown costumes and dunces' caps. This type of entertainment owed its popularity to the runaway success of the London production of the mime play 'L'Enfant Prodigue' in 1891, in which the character of Pierrot featured. The act would feature songs, jokes, mime and monologues.

ABERYSTWYTH CASTLE 1921 71524
During the English Civil War, Aberystwyth was held for the King
until it was surrendered by Colonel Rice Powell in April 1646;
this left Raglan and Harlech as the only castles in Wales held by
the Royalists. During the war the castle had also served as a
mint. Here, silver from nearby mines owned by the ardent
Royalist Thomas Bushell was turned into much-needed coinage.
On 3 March 1647, by order of the Commons, Aberystwyth and
Abergavenny were both ordered to be disgarrisoned prior to
demolition. In July 1649 Aberystwyth was ordered to be blown
up; it became one of a number of fortresses to suffer severe
slighting. Others included Nottingham,
Montgomery and Bolingbroke.

BARRY CASTLE 1899 43454

There is no known record of the history or appearance of this castle, which is situated eight miles south-west of Cardiff. Barry is thought to have been a 14th-century fortified manorial residence; but all that remained in 1899 was the ivy-clad ruins of a small gatehouse or barbican and a section of curtain wall. As can be seen here, the ruins had been incorporated into a farm building.

BEAUMARIS CASTLE GATEWAY 1911 63302

The southern gateway of the outer bailey once guarded a small dock situated where the moat met a channel dug from the sea. Construction of the hexagonal outer bailey curtain wall, its associated towers and gates began in about 1315, though the northern gateway is thought not to have been completed. The design included offsetting the gateways in such a way that any attackers would be forced to turn a corner before reaching the inner ward gate-houses, thus subjecting them to a murderous crossfire from nearby towers.

BEAUMARIS CASTLE 1911 63307
This was the last of Edward Longshanks' Welsh fortresses.
Construction began in 1295 under the personal supervision of
the King's engineer-architect Master James of St George. Master
James used Harlech as the basis for the design, employing two
large gatehouses instead of a keep. The walls were 15ft thick,
and like the gatehouses they were flanked by six towers.
Beaumaris was, in fact, never completed. War with Scotland,
and Longshanks' desire to press his claims in France, meant
that money was tight. The towers of the inner curtain were
never completed to their intended height, and the great hall
and other accommodation and domestic blocks in the inner
ward were never begun.

CAERGWRLE CASTLE c1955 C363044

Situated six miles south-east of Mold, Caergwrle is a small castle comprising the ruins of three round towers and a polygonal turret; it was captured and destroyed in 1282. It sits in one corner of what is thought to be an old hill fort, and was the last castle to be built by a native Welsh prince, Dafydd, brother of Llywelyn ap Gruffydd, Prince of Wales. Dafydd sparked off the revolt of 1282 by taking Hawarden Castle. The following year he was betrayed to the English, captured, and taken to Shrewsbury, where he was hung, drawn and quartered.

CAERNARVON CASTLE 1921 70782
This view looks towards the Eagle Tower. The tower, which is considered by many to be a keep, was possibly built as a residence for Sir Otto de Grandison (1238-1328), the first justiciar of North Wales. He was a close and trusted friend of Edward I, and was also appointed constable of Caernarvon, a post he held for about four years. The fourth storey, battlements and turrets were added to the Eagle Tower in 1317. In 1620 the castle was in such a run-down state that only the Eagle Tower and the King's Tower were roofed.

CAERNARVON CASTLE c1890 C33501

Here we get a good view of the banded masonry along the south front. Inspired by the Theodosian Wall at Constantinople, its use at Caernarvon was deliberate and designed to impress. No one was left in any doubt, especially the Welsh, that they were looking upon the seat of a new royal government and a new imperial power. From left to right the towers are the Eagle; the Queen's; the Chamberlain; and the Black. When the fortress was first built, the waters of the River Seiont lapped these southern walls.

CAERNARVON CASTLE 1890 23116

We are looking west towards the Eagle Tower, with the Queen's and Chamberlain Towers on the left. Between these latter towers once stood the 100ft-long Great Hall, which probably had a buttery and a pantry at its east end. There was direct access between the hall and the Chamberlain Tower, as well as steps leading down to a postern opening towards the Seiont.

CAERNARVON CASTLE 1890 23122

This view looks east. On the left is the King's Gate, on the right the Chamberlain Tower. The high curtain wall enabled Caernarvon to be provided with three levels of defence, ie two levels of casemates and the wall walk. Some of the embrasures were designed so as to allow bowmen to shoot in several directions from the same position. The kitchens, which were largely half-timbered, once stood against the curtain wall in the area of ground to the left of the picture and in front of the King's Gate.

CAERNARVON CASTLE, QUEEN'S GATE 1890 23123

The elevated entrance to the Queen's Gate was due to the fact that behind it lay the motte of the 11th-century castle built by Hugh de Lupus, Earl of Chester. The Queen's Gate led directly into the royal inner ward and was approached by means of a ramp and drawbridge.

CAERNARVON CASTLE 1890 23115
The King's Gate was the entrance to the inner or lower bailey. This side of the castle was defended by a moat; there was once a drawbridge where the steps and stone bridge appear in this picture. The passageway of the King's Gate was protected by five doors, six portcullises, arrow loops, and murder holes in the vaulted ceiling. The upper floor was used as a chapel. There were plans to build a hall above that, but the work was never completed.

CAERNARVON, THE TOWN WALL 1906 54827

Simultaneous construction of the castle and town wall began in the summer of 1283. The wall, which enclosed the medieval borough, is 800 yds long with eight towers and two twin-towered gateways. The wall formed three sides of the town defences, from the north-east Tower round to the Eagle Tower; the fourth side was provided by the north curtain of the castle. The tower nearest the camera had been remodelled in the 19th century and was occupied when this picture was taken. The next tower along is the west gate; it has a small barbican to its front. The farthest tower was also in use, being occupied by the local authority.

CAERPHILLY CASTLE c1955 C5122

This view shows Caerphilly following the restoration both of its fabric and its water defences by the Marquis of Bute. The principal residential block, which included the great hall, was situated along the south side of the inner curtain wall. The drum towers at the angles of the inner curtain were also used for accommodation, and the constable's apartments were in the east gatehouse. In the centre of the curtain of the outer ward is the south water gate; there might also have been one on the north side, but alas no trace remains. The wall going off picture to the right is part of the fortified dam.

CAERPHILLY CASTLE c1874 7032
Gilbert de Clare's second attempt to build a castle at Caerphilly got under way in 1271, his previous unfinished castle having been destroyed by Llywelyn in 1268. This castle too was attacked by Llywelyn; this forced Henry III to intervene and declare Caerphilly neutral territory. However, de Clare had the backing of the barons and retook his own castle by force, forcing the Welsh to withdraw.

CAERPHILLY CASTLE 1871 7033
The construction of Caerphilly and its associated water defences must have been a drain on resources, even for a man as wealthy as Gilbert de Clare. De Clare had an income estimated to be in the region of £5500 to £6000 a year. Even so, he would not have seen much change from between £7500 and £11,000.

CAERPHILLY CASTLE 1893 32707

Here we see the fortified dam prior to restoration. If you look to the extreme left of it you can just make out the south water gate, which at this time was high and dry. The water defences extended to this side of the dam.

CARDIFF CASTLE 1893 32670

The first Norman castle at Cardiff is thought to have been built in c1081, possibly on the site of a Welsh stronghold. Robert FitzHamon chose to build his castle within the ruins of the old Roman fortress, raising a motte in the north-west corner. Additional protection came by digging out the original Roman ditch defences and piling the spoil over what remained of the circuit walls to create a rampart.

CARDIFF CASTLE 1893 32672
The east face of the castle was rebuilt in a lavish romantic-Gothic style by John Patrick Crichton-Stuart, Third Marquess of Bute. As with his rebuilding of Castell Coch, the marquess was influenced by continental styles.

CARDIFF CASTLE 1893 32669

It was to Cardiff Castle that Robert Curthose, Duke of Normandy, was brought after his defeat at Tinchebrai in 1106, having made war on both William Rufus and Henry I. Curthose's eyes were put out and he remained a prisoner until his death in 1134.

CARREG CENNEN CASTLE 1936 87715A

Standing on a 300 ft limestone crag overlooking the Towy Valley, the present Carreg Cennen dates from the late 13th century, though the site has historical links with the ancient commote of Is-Cennen, and sections of the south and west curtain walls might date from a castle held by Rhys Fychan in the 1240s. Late 13th-century work includes the gatehouse to the inner ward and the chapel tower; the barbican and outer ward are later. The castle was slighted by Yorkists during the Wars of The Roses.

CASTELL COCH c1960 T188003
Castell Coch has featured in a number of films, both for screen and television. The present building dates from 1870; it is a romantic reconstruction of a medieval fortress designed by William Burges for John Patrick Crichton-Stuart, Third Marquess of Bute. Of the two previous castles on the site, the first was a short-lived motte and bailey erected when the Normans pushed into the Cardiff area. The second was a small, well-designed de Clare stronghold, which seems to have lasted only a couple of hundred years before being abandoned and deliberately destroyed.

CASTELL DINAS BRAN 1913 65824A

The Hill of Bran rises just to the north-east of Llangollen; perched high upon its summit is the ruin of Castell Dinas Bran. This is where Gruffydd ap Madoc withdrew after giving his support to the English Crown against the Welsh. Built out of local shale and slate, the castle is thought to have been built by Madoc in about 1236, though it could be earlier.

CASTELL DINAS BRAN 1901 47224

The site occupied by Castell Dinas Bran may have been fortified as early as the 8th century. The ruins include a large shell keep within a rectangular ward, a twin-towered gatehouse, a large D-shaped tower, and traces of a hall. There are traces of what might be a barbican or a small ward separated from the gate by a ditch. The ditch gave additional protection to the side of the castle thought most vulnerable to a frontal assault.

CHEPSTOW CASTLE 1893 32495

The original castle at Chepstow was begun by William Fitz Osbern in 1067. The site chosen was a
long narrow ridge high above the River Wye. Fitz Osbern built a long rectangular fortified hall
(the Great Tower) on the narrowest part of the ridge. A two-storey structure, it features pilasters
and a string course of re-used Roman tiles, and its walls are only 3 - 6ft thick - keep walls are usually
between 8 and 20 ft thick. Fitz Osbern protected his hall by means of a stone curtain wall on all
four sides; the defensive capability of the three landward sides was enhanced by a ditch.

CHEPSTOW CASTLE
Marten's Tower 1893 32498

Marten's Tower is named after the regicide Henry Marten (1602-80) who was imprisoned in it in fairly comfortable conditions for twenty years until his death in 1680. Marten had been one of the signatories to the death warrant of Charles I, and as such faced almost certain death himself at the Restoration of Charles II. His life, however, was spared. This might be due to the fact that the ultra-Republican Marten had become convinced that Cromwell really did want to be crowned king. This led to a serious rift between the two men, and Marten became an outspoken opponent of the Lord Protector and all his works.

CHEPSTOW CASTLE, MARTEN'S TOWER 1893 32496

Marten's Tower and its flanking turrets was erected between 1285 and 1293 by Roger Bigod III. The tower is a massive D-shaped structure protected at ground level from attack either from battering ram or undermining by two spur bastions. The tower performed a dual function. Militarily, it enabled flank fire to be directed against attackers attempting an assault upon the barbican and twin-towered gatehouse. Domestically, it formed the private apartments of Roger Bigod.

CHIRK CASTLE c1869 5519

The present castle was begun in about 1283 by Roger Mortimer. There had been an earlier marcher stronghold at Chirk; it was either on this site or nearer to the village, where traces of a motte and bailey survive, but wherever it was it had long fallen into disrepair. When built, Chirk was an Edwardian square castle with a drum-tower at each angle, though by 1310 work was under way to extend it. The battlements were wide enough for two men to walk along side-by-side, and a principal feature was the castle's 160ft x 100ft quadrangle, the entrance to which can be seen in this picture between two drum-towers.

CHIRK CASTLE c1955

One of Chirk's more unusual claims to fame is that it was once besieged by its owner. During the first English Civil War it was garrisoned for the King, though its owner, Thomas Myddelton, was fighting for Parliament. Thomas laid siege to Chirk, but was unable to take it. At the end of the war it was returned to him, but he changed sides when the second Civil War broke out; he found himself besieged at Chirk by a Parliamentarian force commanded by General Lambert.

CHIRK CASTLE c1955

These splendid decorative iron gates were made by the Davies brothers of Bersham between 1719 and 1721.

CHIRK CASTLE c1955 C366118

COITY CASTLE 1899 43353
Coity Castle stands less than two miles to the north-east of
Bridgend. There is a legend of how Payn de Turberville
acquired Coity following the Norman conquest of Glamorgan.
For services rendered, Payn expected to be awarded lands, but
was told to go off and find his own. He arrived outside Coity,
liked the look of the place and demanded that the Welsh chief-
tain, Morgan, immediately surrender it to him. Morgan not only
rode out ready for battle, he also brought along his not-unat-
tractive daughter Sybil. It was Payn who was given a choice. He
could fight, and possibly die, or he could wed Sybil and inherit
Coity. Payn chose the latter and the couple were soon married.
Payn swore allegiance to Caradoc ap Jestyn, and his descendants
lived at Coity until the end of the 14th century, when the male
line of de Turberville became extinct.

COITY CASTLE 1898 41202

To the left of the castle stands Coity Church. It is noted for two 14th-century monuments to de Turberville children, and a legged oak gabled coffer upon which are carved scenes from the Passion. The earliest castle ruins date from the 12th century, and include the keep and curtain wall of the inner ward. The bulk of the ruins, however, are from the 14th century and Tudor periods.

CONWY CASTLE 1913 65754

This view looks towards the inner ward. The King's apartments were on the first floor. Here was the Presence Chamber, where Councils would have been held. There was a smaller chamber for more private business, a chapel, and a lobby for guests to wait in before being received. The towers at the angle of the castle contained bedchambers for use by the King and Queen. On the ground floor were apartments for the King's officials.

CONWY CASTLE c1960 C156272
In this picture we see most of Conwy's drum-towers, each of which is almost identical in size and plan. All the towers were originally surmounted with round turrets, but only those on the inner ward towers have survived.

CONWY CASTLE 1913 65753
Because the curtain walls were so high, there were large areas of dead ground around the fortress that the defenders were unable to fire to into with any accuracy. The north and west curtains faced the town and were considered vulnerable to assault should the town fall. The north curtain's defensive capability was enhanced by six embrasures at ground floor level. These enabled archers to fire upon any attackers attempting a direct assault upon the north curtain, and allowed them to target a section of the town wall. The west curtain was protected by its own barbican.

CONWY CASTLE 1898 42386

In March 1283 Longshanks ordered Conwy Castle to be built and a burgh established. The choosing of the site was deliberate: here was the royal hall of Llywelyn the Great (demolished 1316) and the Cistercian Abbey of St Mary where he lay buried. For Longshanks, there was symbolism in not only ordering the abbey dismantled, but to having it re-erected at Maenan eight miles away.

CONWY CASTLE 1890 26794

We are looking across the estuary towards the inner ward. The picture gives us an idea of just how steep the ridge is upon which the castle is built. The slope of the rock on the south side was such that it would have been impossible to mount an assault from that direction using battering rams or siege towers. Also, the curtain wall was too high for the scaling ladders of the day.

CRICCIETH CASTLE 1931 84766

Criccieth was a Welsh fortress, and was probably completed in the early 13th century by Llywelyn ap Iorwerth. It was captured by the English early in 1283, who immediately set about improving its defensive capability; Edward Longshanks committed a great deal of money to the project. Further work was carried out between 1287 and 1288, and the towers were heightened during the reign of Edward II. Criccieth became something of a hybrid: an Edwardian inner ward inside what was essentially a Welsh outer ward. In 1326 the garrison stood at ten men; their main defensive weapon was the crossbow. It fired a heavy, hard-hitting bolt that could penetrate armour at ranges up to 250 yds.

CRICKHOWELL CASTLE 1893 32609

CRICKHOWELL CASTLE 1893

Crickhowell Castle lies twelve miles south-east of Brecon. Originally it was a timber stronghold of the motte and bailey, and belonged to the de Turberville family. When rebuilt in stone it featured both a shell keep and a shell gatehouse.

CYFARTHFA CASTLE c1955

Not so much a castle as a huge castellated mansion, Cyfarthfa stands near Merthyr Tydfil and was built in 1825 for Robert Thomas Crawshay, a wealthy ironmaster. Crawshay, like Francis Frith, was an early devotee of photography.

CYFARTHFA CASTLE c1955 M118038

DENBIGH CASTLE 1888 20853

Work on Denbigh began in October 1282 during the second of Edward I's Welsh Wars. It was not a royal fortress, but was built by Henry de Lacy, Earl of Lincoln, though his architect was Master James of St George and Edward I gave support. As with a number of fortresses raised at this time, Denbigh was deliberately built on a site that had meaning to the Welsh - in this instance a former royal residence of the princes of Gwynedd.

DENBIGH CASTLE c1885 17805

During the revolt of 1294 the Welsh won a victory at Denbigh: it is unclear as to whether this refers to a pitched battle, taking the castle, or the town, or any combination of these three. The English were soon back, and work continued on the castle, but it stopped again a few years later when Henry de Lacy, distraught at the death by drowning of his only son in the castle well, wanted nothing more to do with the place. Following de Lacy's death in 1311, the castle passed through a number of hands.

DENBIGH CASTLE 1888 20851

Here we see the remains of the great triple-towered gatehouse. It is thought that Edward I's engineer-architect Master James of St George was responsible for its design. The towers were arranged two at the front and one at the rear, thus creating a small octagonal courtyard in the middle of them. This sounds very attractive, but any attackers reaching this point would be caught in a vicious crossfire from murder holes. The gatehouse was also defended by two portcullises and two doors.

DENBIGH CASTLE 1888 20854

Throughout the First Civil War, both town and castle were held by the Royalists, and as such was one of the last to surrender. In March 1647 Parliament ordered the withdrawal of its garrison, though slighting did not begin in earnest until 1660 when gunpowder was used. In the 19th century a walled-up chamber in the west gate was opened and found to be full of gunpowder.

DENBIGH CASTLE
The Goblin Tower c1885

It was from the top of the Goblin Tower that the keys to the castle and town were hurled at the feet of the Parliamentarian commander Major General Mytton upon the surrender of the Royalist garrison.

DENBIGH CASTLE c1960

Denbigh saw action during the Wars of The Roses and changed hands on several occasions. In 1468 it finally fell to a Lancastrian force led by Jasper Tewdwr, Earl of Pembroke. Both town and castle were put to the torch; the damage to the former was such that when reconstruction started much of the town was built outside the old walls.

DENBIGH CASTLE, THE GOBLIN TOWER c1885 17807

DENBIGH CASTLE c1960 D22106

DOLWYDDELAN CASTLE 1891 29541

Five miles south-west of Betwys-y-Coed, Dolwyddelan Castle was founded about
1170 by Iorwerth Trwyndwn (the Flatnosed), and this was where his son Llywelyn
was born. The castle was strategically sited so as to control the principal route
between Nant Conway and Meirionnydd by way of the Lledr Valley, and was
Iorwerth's home for many years. It was captured by the English in January 1283
following the death of Llywelyn the Last.

DOLWYDDELAN CASTLE 1891 29542
It has been argued that Dolwyddelan was not Iorwerth's castle at all, and that the honour should in fact be bestowed upon nearby Tomen Castell; here, there are the remains of a rectangular tower. The surviving rectangular tower at Dolwyddelan is thought to have been built as late as 1270, possibly by Llywelyn ap Gruffydd as a two-storey structure. A third storey was added in the 15th century.

DUNRAVEN CASTLE c1955 S156016

Situated five miles south-west of Bridgend, the Dunraven in our picture is the 19th-century castellated mansion built for Thomas Wyndham MP between 1802 and 1806 on the site of a medieval fortress. The original design for Dunraven was based on Clearwell Castle, Gloucestershire, which was also owned by Wyndham. The picture is looking towards the palm court.

DUNRAVEN CASTLE c1955 S156022

The door, two-seater sofa, tables and chairs give us a clue as to just how large the palm court was.

DUNRAVEN CASTLE 1901 47926

In this view we can see the squat tower and castellated wing designed by George Devey for Lord Dunraven and built in 1886-88. Lord Dunraven spent much of his time on his estate at Adare, Ireland, and it was while he was on a trip to see his lordship that Devey died after contracting a chill. Devey's assistant Isaac Williams took over the project, though the work continued to be based on Devey's sketches.

DUNRAVEN CASTLE C1955 O72039

For his defence of Ogmore Castle against the Welsh, Arnold de Boteler was awarded the manor of Dunraven by William de Londres. Eventually the manor passed by marriage to the Vaughan family; several members of that family were apt to engage in a little freelance wrecking of ships in order to seize their cargoes. It was a usual custom amongst wreckers to kill any sailors who had survived the wrecking; after all, dead men tell no tales. The Vaughans are said to have given up the practice when they wrecked a ship captained by one of their own family.

FLINT CASTLE c1955 F120040

The construction of Flint Castle began within days of the signing of the treaty of Rhuddlan; it was the first of the Edwardian fortresses built to impose a new order upon Wales. Work began in the summer of 1277 on both the castle and a new borough; the English had come to colonize as well as conquer. The borough was given a ditch and palisade, the castle was built in stone from the start.

FLINT CASTLE c1955 F120019

Flint was given a large but weak outer bailey, but the rectangular inner ward was supported with towers at the angles. The south-east tower, or donjon, had walls 23 ft thick and was separated from the wall of the inner ward by its own moat and drawbridge.

FLINT CASTLE c1955 F120021

This picture shows the ruin of the donjon. The curtain wall was
once a lot higher, but was reduced when the castle was slighted
during the English Civil War. In 1399 Richard II was brought
here after being intercepted by the Earl of Northumberland.
Richard had returned from Ireland, landing at Milford Haven,
and was on his way to Conway to suppress a rebellion and meet
up with his cousin Henry Bolingbroke. Henry had other ideas;
he wanted the throne for himself, and had the support of a
number of lords including Northumberland. Richard was per-
suaded to ride to Flint with only a small personal escort of five
esquires, and Northumberland was lying in wait for him.
Richard was eventually taken to Pontefract Castle where he
died, either murdered or starved to death.

FONMON CASTLE 1899 43464

Founded in c1200, Fonmon is thought to have comprised two round towers, a square tower or keep and a curtain wall. Parts of this castle were absorbed into a mansion house built on the site during the late 17th century.

FONMON CASTLE 1899 43465

Fonmon underwent further rebuilding in the 18th century and was repaired during the 19th century. The castle appears to have no recorded history.

GWYRCH CASTLE 1891 29170

During the late 18th and early 19th centuries a large number of country houses were built in the castellated style. Some, like Brancepeth in Northumberland, were built to replace what had been fortresses; others, like Gwyrch, were new construction on virgin sites. Gwyrch, one mile west of Abergele, was completed in 1815. Many of its towers were built for show and serve no purpose whatsoever.

HALKYN CASTLE c1955 H286009
Situated a few miles south-east of Holywell, Halkyn is not really a castle but a castellated country house, one of a number once owned by the Dukes of Westminster.

HARLECH CASTLE 1889 21737
The twin-towered gatehouse, or Le Gemeltour Supra Portram as it was called in a survey of the castle undertaken in 1343, is flanked on the right by the Prison Tower (Le Prisontour), and on the left by the Garden Tower (Turris Ultra Gardinum). In the Prison Tower a trap-door in the floor of the first floor was the only way in, or out, of a deep circular dungeon. A similar room also existed in the basement of the Garden Tower.

HARLECH CASTLE 1894 34682

When Harlech was built, the sea lapped around the base of the
rocky crag upon which it stands. At sea level there was the water
gate, which allowed the fortress to be reinforced or supplied by
ship. Any attacker capturing the water gate then faced a climb
of 108 steps up the side of the crag to the next objective, an
intermediate turret with a drawbridge. Attackers also had to run
the gauntlet of artillery fire, possibly from trebuchets, mounted
on platforms near to the castle. These weapons, when handled
by experienced crews, could be fired accurately.

HARLECH CASTLE 1889 21736
In this view from the south-west, two smallish levelled areas that appear to be stepped one above the other can be seen to the left of the castle. These are the artillery platforms mentioned in the caption to photograph No 34682. The weapons deployed on them were probably mounted trebuchets, positioned to give supporting fire to the defenders of the Water Gate.

HARLECH CASTLE 1933 85641
Additional protection was given to the eastern and southern
flanks of Harlech by a deep ditch. Entry to the castle was by way
of the twin-towered main gatehouse on the eastern side. The
approach to this was in turn defended by an outer gatehouse
with corbelled turrets and a drawbridge, plus two bridge turrets
which spanned the ditch. The passageway defences of the main
gatehouse were impressive. To reach the inner courtyard attackers had to breach an outer wooden door, two portcullises, a second wooden door and a third portcullis, whilst running a gauntlet of crossbow bolts and arrows fired
through loops by the garrison.

HAVERFORDWEST CASTLE 1890 27940

It is thought that Gilbert de Clare fortified the site in the early 12th century, but the ruins seen here date from the stronghold built by Walter de Valence in the 13th century. The castle withstood attacks from Llywelyn the Great and Owain Glyndwr only to be slighted by Parliament in 1646.

KIDWELLY CASTLE 1893 32800

Standing on rising ground on the west bank of the River Gwendraeth, Kidwelly and its fortified town were founded by Roger, Bishop of Salisbury during the reign of Henry I. The present castle dates from c1275 when it was begun by Payn de Charworth and completed by Henry of Lancaster. The picture shows the southern gatehouse, and it was here on the first and second floors that the constable had his apartments. The machicolation above the gateway dates from remodelling carried out by Henry IV. Not visible in this picture is the sweeping arc of the superb outer curtain wall built by Henry of Lancaster.

LLANDAFF CASTLE c1955 L67078

LLANDAFF CASTLE c1955

The ruined gatehouse of Llandaff Castle was probably built in the early 14th century, though it was remodelled a couple of hundred years later when mullion and transomed windows were installed in its western tower. Llandaff is said to have been destroyed c1402 by Owain Glyndwr.

MARGAM CASTLE 1936

Designed by Thomas Hopper and Edward Haycock for C R Mansel-Talbot, Margam was the subject in some of Fox-Talbot's earliest photographs. Mansel-Talbot was a noted collector of works of art and amassed what was perhaps the finest private collection in Wales. When it was sold off in 1941, there were 464 pictures and 995 lots of furniture.

MARGAM CASTLE 1936 87738

LLANSTEPHAN CASTLE c1955 L79019

This view was taken from Plas Field. The stronghold passed to William de Camville on his marriage to Albreda, daughter of Geoffrey Marmion, the first recorded lord of Llanstephan. It would remain in the de Camville family until the male line died out in 1338. It was captured and held briefly by the Lord Rhys in 1189, an episode that led de Camville into strengthening its defences and replacing wood with stone

LLANSTEPHAN CASTLE 1893 32794

Llanstephan is a double enclosure castle of the 12th and 13th centuries. Its defences on three sides were enhanced by natural scarping, while the fourth was given a double ditch. There is some confusion as to just how old the castle is, as references to it being burnt by Welsh raiders in 1137 might in fact relate to Castell Stephan near Lampeter.

LLANSTEPHAN CASTLE 1893 32798

The fortress is irregular in outline, as its builders decided to follow the contours of the land. Various de Camvilles added to the castle. The great gatehouse and mural towers of the outer ward were probably built during the reign of Henry III. A large-scale reconstruction was begun by the second William de Camville and continued by his son, the second Geoffrey. During this period the gatehouse was remodelled to become a keep.

MANORBIER CASTLE 1890 27985

MANORBIER CASTLE 1890

The first castle at Manorbier was probably a motte and bailey erected by Odo de Barri. The castle underwent large-scale remodelling and extension over a fifty-year period during the 13th century, much of the work being commissioned by John de Barri.

MANORBIER CASTLE 1890

The de Barris held Manorbier for two hundred years until 1399, when it was declared forfeit to the Crown owing to Sir David de Barri having supported Richard II. The earliest remains in stone are a hall and a small tower, both of which date from the 12th century. A famous resident from the 12th century was Gerald de Barri, born here in 1146, and better known to us as Giraldus Cambrensis, the author of the 'Itinerary of Wales'.

MANORBIER CASTLE 1890 27981

Monmouth Castle 1896 38693

Here we see the overgrown and sadly-neglected ruin of
Monmouth Castle as it looked in 1893. The fortress was built by
William Fitz Osbern between 1067 and 1071, and was one of a
chain of strongholds erected to hold down south-east Wales. By
1100 it was an important place, the seat of the Marcher
Lordship of Monmouth. The title was then held by William Fitz
Baderon, and it would remain in his family for over 150 years.
When the last of the male line of the Fitz Baderons died, the
castle was bequeathed to no less a person than Prince Edward,
the son of Henry III; as Edward I he would become perhaps the
most capable and yet most ruthless king ever to sit on the
throne of England. Whilst in Prince Edward's possession,
Monmouth was attacked and taken by Simon de Montfort,
though Edward soon regained it. In 1267 it was given to
Edward's younger brother Edmund Crouchback, Earl of
Lancaster. It was here in 1387 that the future
King Henry V was born.

NEWPORT CASTLE 1893 32631

Founded in 1172, Newport was heavily rebuilt during the 14th and 15th centuries. The picture shows the surviving curtain wall facing the River Usk. In the centre is the square gate tower with its arched water gate. Boats could enter the castle through the water gate, as there was a small quay to the rear of the tower. Double gates controlled the water level under the tower, and unwelcome visitors trying to gain access by this route would have to get through two portcullises.

OGMORE CASTLE 1901 47908
Situated two miles south-south-west of Bridgend, Ogmore was
originally a ringwork with a timber palisade built in 1116 by
William de Londres to guard crossing points on the rivers
Ewenny and Ogmore. The stronghold formed an integral part
of the defences of the western border of Glamorgan, which also
included the castles of Newcastle at Bridgend and Coity.

OGMORE CASTLE 1898 41217

Here was built one of the earliest stone keeps in Wales, a rectangular affair of two storeys, later raised to three. As our picture shows, the ivy-clad ruins were still standing over 40 ft high in 1898.

OGMORE CASTLE 1937 87885

After the castle came into the ownership of the Ministry of Works in 1927, the ivy was cleared away. Here we get a good view of the remains of the early 12th-century keep which was built so as to flank the entrance to the inner ward. The palisade was replaced by a stone curtain wall in the early 13th century.

OXWICH CASTLE 1910 62598

In 1541 a large manor house was constructed within the remnants of the old castle. It even incorporated a part of the curtain wall, gatehouse and great tower. Above the gate can be seen the arms of Sir Rhys Mansell (1487-1559), who by the reign of Queen Mary had become one of Glamorgan's chief landowners.

OXWICH CASTLE c1955 O38011

Oxwich was Sir Rhys's main residence. He was certainly a man of his time; he was a veteran of the wars in Ireland, Chamberlain of Chester, and a member of the Council in the Marches. Between 1542 and 1546 he served in the wars against France and Scotland. Though he appears to have been out of favour during the reign of Edward VI, he returned to prominence upon the accession of Queen Mary with his appointment as chamberlain and chancellor for the south of Wales.

OXWICH CASTLE 1910 62599

At Christmas 1557, Oxwich would be the scene of an incident that would result in litigation before the Court of the Star Chamber. Sir Rhys was distantly related to Sir George Herbert (?1498-1570), another wealthy landowner and vice-Admiral of the Crown. The trouble started over the cargo of a French merchant ship wrecked on Oxwich Point. Sir George intended to hold an inquiry to access ownership of the spoils, and sent two retainers ahead to secure the cargo. They had no warrant, so Sir Rhys's tenants refused to hand anything over. The whole episode got totally out of hand and ended in the death of Anne Mansell, who had ridden over to Oxwich with the intention of acting as the family peacemaker.

OYSTERMOUTH CASTLE 1893 32737

Following its destruction during the rising of 1287, Oystermouth was rebuilt as a courtyard castle. At one end was a three-storey gatehouse whose top floor was occupied by a large chapel. At the other end was the rectangular tower, the remains of which are the subject of photograph No 32739. These two structures were linked together by high curtain walls. Remodelling went on into the 16th century. The castle might have been provided with some sort of outer defence, such as a palisade.

OYSTERMOUTH CASTLE 1893 32739

Situated four miles south-west of Swansea overlooking Swansea Bay, Oystermouth derives its name from a Norman/English corruption of Ystmllwynarth. The first stronghold on the site was probably built by Henry Beaumont, Earl of Warwick, following his being made Lord of Gower by Henry I. Oystermouth was captured by the Lord Rhys, but was later handed over to John de Braose by Llywelyn the Great.

PEMBROKE CASTLE 1890 27955

William Marshall's great cylindrical keep towers above the ruins.
Built in the late 12th and early 13th centuries, the keep performed
both residential and military roles. Its walls were the same thickness
all the way up, which enhanced its defensive capabilities. However
this may have inhibited the design of the two floors of residential
apartments - though not the quality of their fittings. The top floor
of the keep was primarily a fighting platform. It is, however, unlikely
that the apartments were to be used except as a retreat of last resort,
as the keep lacked a well and there were no garderobes.

PEMBROKE CASTLE 1890 27957

Without doubt, Pembroke is one of the most impressive defended sites in Wales. The first castle was built by Roger de Montgomery and his son, possibly on the site of a native Welsh fortification or fortified settlement. Pembroke was taken by Roger in 1093, during what can only be described as a scramble by Norman lords to help themselves to the lands of the recently murdered Rhys ap Tewdwr.

PEMBROKE CASTLE c1955 P22128
Construction of the outer ward was begun by William de
Valence around 1260 and continued under Aymer de Valence.
In shape it would form an irregular hexagon, with a tower at
each of the angles. There was also a large gatehouse protected
by a barbican, and the landward sides of the curtain wall were
given a ditch defence. From left to right we see the Westgate
Tower, the Henry VII Tower, the Great Gatehouse, and the
Barbican Tower. The ruined wall is the remains of the barbican. In January 1457, the future Henry VII is said to have been
born in one of the rooms of the gatehouse.

PENNARD CASTLE 1893 32760

Pennard stands high above a tidal creek some eight miles west-
south-west of Swansea. The ruins are of a late 13th-century rectangular castle built on the site of an earlier stronghold that was
possibly destroyed during the Lord Rhys' campaign. There is a
twin-towered gatehouse to the landward side, and square towers
at each corner of the curtain wall. There is little information as
to who owned Pennard, or who even lived in it. There is no evidence for any 15th- or 16th-century rebuilding work, so the castle might well have been abandoned
during the 14th century.

PENRHYN CASTLE 1890 23130
One mile east of Bangor off the present-day A55
stands Penrhyn Castle, a popular attraction with visitors to the area. Penrhyn, however, is not an old
fortress, but a Victorian country house built on the
grand scale. It was designed by Thomas Hopper for
Dawkins Pennant, heir to a vast fortune made
in the Welsh slate industry.

PENRHYN CASTLE 1890 23129

No expense was spared in creating Penrhyn, though local materials were used where practical. The marble came from Anglesey, timber from Pennant's estates, and slate from his own quarries.

PENRICE CASTLE 1910 62593

The earliest castle was an earthwork and timber fortification at Mounty Brough, built soon after the Normans had taken the Gower. The construction of Penrice took place over about fifty years, beginning in c1250 with a stone round keep, followed by curtain wall, gatehouse, two round towers and five small turrets.

PENRICE CASTLE c1955 P32018
A corner of the 13th-century castle can be seen at the top right
of the picture, though our main subject is the country house
built by Thomas Mansel Talbot in the 1770s and its 19th-century
additions. A stone-faced wing by William Powell was added
between 1812 and 1817, and the last building phase was the
block erected between 1893 and 1896. The front also sported
an ornate iron and glass conservatory by Macfarlane's of
Glasgow, but this was removed after the Second World War.
Further demolition was undertaken during 1967-68.

RAGLAN CASTLE 1906 54516
In the 1460s William Herbert set about
remodelling Raglan in the contemporary
French style. These features included a tower-
keep separated from the rest of the castle by
its own moat, multiangular towers, and ornate
machicolations of the type seen here adorn-
ing the tops of the hexagonal corner towers
of the gatehouse. The circular gun-ports at
the base of the gatehouse walls are obscured
by hedging.

RAGLAN CASTLE 1893 32534

RAGLAN CASTLE 1893 32531

RAGLAN CASTLE 1893

William Herbert's tower-keep is seen here on the right of the picture. The building was designed to take account of the latest thinking in military architecture; Raglan was primarily a fortress, not a stately home. The keep was isolated from the rest of the castle by its own moat, and defended by a double drawbridge.

RAGLAN CASTLE 1893

Here we see the gatehouse and the moat of the tower-keep. As a professional soldier, William Herbert had fought for and been knighted by Henry VI. It was, however, his unwavering support for Edward IV at Mortimer's Cross in 1461 that earned him the title of Baron Herbert. Other honours were to follow. In 1462 he was created a Knight of the Garter, and in 1468 he was created earl of Pembroke as reward for taking Harlech Castle and capturing both Jasper Twdwr and Prince Henry (later Henry VII).

RAGLAN CASTLE 1893 32532

Raglan was not divided into wards but into two courts, the Stone and the Fountain. These are in turn separated from one another by what was a 60ft high building that included the great hall (66ft x 28ft), the earl's private dining room, a large buttery, a withdrawing room, and the great gallery.

RAGLAN CASTLE 1893 32533

The Fountain Court housed the castle's state apartments. Charles I visited the castle after his defeat at the hands of the New Model Army at Naseby on 14 June 1645, arriving on 3 July from Abergavenny. The King was still at Raglan on 22 July when he received the news that Goring had been defeated at Langport by Fairfax and Cromwell.

RAGLAN CASTLE 1931 83798
We are looking towards the Kitchen Tower, which is situated in the Stone Court. The main entrance to this court was by a gatehouse protected by a portcullis.

RHUDDLAN CASTLE c1955 R334004

Situated three miles south of Rhyl, Rhuddlan was once a strategic location, as it was the lowest point at which the Clwyd could be crossed. The place had been fortified since the 8th century; in the 11th century it was the stronghold of Gruffydd ap Llywelyn, though it was destroyed by Harold Godwinsson in 1063. A motte and bailey was built here in the early 1070s by Robert de Rhuddlan, but the ruins we see today date back to the fortress of Edward I.

ROCH CASTLE c1955 R293014

ROCH CASTLE c1955

Built by Adam de Rupe in the second half of the 13th century, Roch is noted for its distinctive D-shaped tower. The legend is that de Rupe built his castle here in order that he might escape a prophecy that he would die from the bite of a viper. Alas for Adam, a viper found its way into the castle; it had hidden in a bundle of firewood, and the prophecy was fulfilled.

ST FAGAN'S CASTLE 1893

In the 16th century St Fagan's Castle was rebuilt as a Tudor mansion. There was an earlier castle on the site, but little is known about it save for traces of what might be a 13th-century curtain wall. Set in 98 acres of parkland, St Fagan's was donated for use as a National Museum by the Earl of Plymouth and now houses the Welsh National Folk Museum.

ST FAGAN'S CASTLE 1893 32716

ST DONAT'S CASTLE 1937 87913

There are no identifiable remains of the castle built here in the 12th and 13th centuries. St Donat's was rebuilt by Sir William Stradling during the reign of Edward III and remodelled during the Tudor period. The castle is divided into two wards, the outer being defended by a gatehouse with a portcullis. This picture shows the approach to the gatehouse by way of a bridge over the dry ditch defence.

ST DONAT'S CASTLE 1937 87914

A number of Stradling family members fought for King Charles I during the Civil War, including Sir Edward Stradling, who commanded a Welsh regiment at the Battle of Edgehill (23 October 1642), where he was captured. St Donat's was ordered to be slighted in 1646, but was restored by the family in 1660, when Grinling Gibbons was commissioned to supply carvings for the state rooms. The castle underwent further restoration in the 19th centu-

ST DONAT'S CASTLE, THE INNER COURTYARD c1960 W459015

The last of the male line of the Stradling family died in 1738, not of old age in his bed, but killed in a duel at Montpellier whilst on the Grand Tour. The young man's body was brought back to St Donat's, where it lay in state in the great gallery, looked down upon by the portraits of his equally dead ancestors. Unfortunately, the funerary decorations caught fire, and body, portraits, and the great gallery went up in flames.

ST DONAT'S CASTLE 1937 87915
We are looking towards the gatehouse. Many of the windows featured in these pictures date from remodelling undertaken during the Tudor and Jacobean periods. The late 19th-century work by Bodley was of such high standard and blended in so well that it is now difficult to identify. The circular patch of light stone on the gatehouse is where a clock face used to be.

ST DONAT'S CASTLE, THE TUDOR GARDENS 1910 62537
The south front of St Donat's overlooks the Bristol Channel, and a series of terraced gardens lead down to the shore.

SWANSEA CASTLE 1893 32724

Henry Beaumont, Lord of Gower, built a motte and bailey at Swansea in about 1099; it was destroyed in 1115-1116 and probably not rebuilt. The remains seen here belong to what in effect was a fortified manor house belonging to the Bishops of St David's. It was badly damaged during Owain Glyndwr's rebellion.

WENVOE CASTLE 1899 43468

This is the only country house to be built in Wales that was designed by Robert Adam. Peter Birt, a wealthy Yorkshireman, bought Wenvoe in 1775 and commissioned Adam to rebuild it. The finished design is similar to Mellerstain Castle, Scotland. Our picture was taken eleven years before Wenvoe was so badly damaged by fire that the owners could not afford to restore it. Nearly everything was demolished in c1930, save for one of the pavilions, which went on to enjoy a second career as the club-house for a golf club, and the stable block.

Index

Frith Book Co Titles

www.francisfrith.co.uk

The Frith Book Company publishes over 100 new titles each year. A selection of those currently available is listed below. For latest catalogue please contact Frith Book Co.

Town Books 96 pages, approximately 100 photos. **County and Themed Books** 128 pages, approximately 150 photos (unless specified). All titles hardback with laminated case and jacket, except those indicated pb (paperback)

Amersham, Chesham & Rickmansworth (pb)	1-85937-340-2	£9.99	Devon (pb)	1-85937-297-x	£9.99
Andover (pb)	1-85937-292-9	£9.99	Devon Churches (pb)	1-85937-250-3	£9.99
Aylesbury (pb)	1-85937-227-9	£9.99	Dorchester (pb)	1-85937-307-0	£9.99
Barnstaple (pb)	1-85937-300-3	£9.99	Dorset (pb)	1-85937-269-4	£9.99
Basildon Living Memories (pb)	1-85937-515-4	£9.99	Dorset Coast (pb)	1-85937-299-6	£9.99
Bath (pb)	1-85937-419-0	£9.99	Dorset Living Memories (pb)	1-85937-584-7	£9.99
Bedford (pb)	1-85937-205-8	£9.99	Down the Severn (pb)	1-85937-560-x	£9.99
Bedfordshire Living Memories	1-85937-513-8	£14.99	Down The Thames (pb)	1-85937-278-3	£9.99
Belfast (pb)	1-85937-303-8	£9.99	Down the Trent	1-85937-311-9	£14.99
Berkshire (pb)	1-85937-191-4	£9.99	East Anglia (pb)	1-85937-265-1	£9.99
Berkshire Churches	1-85937-170-1	£17.99	East Grinstead (pb)	1-85937-138-8	£9.99
Berkshire Living Memories	1-85937-332-1	£14.99	East London	1-85937-080-2	£14.99
Black Country	1-85937-497-2	£12.99	East Sussex (pb)	1-85937-606-1	£9.99
Blackpool (pb)	1-85937-393-3	£9.99	Eastbourne (pb)	1-85937-399-2	£9.99
Bognor Regis (pb)	1-85937-431-x	£9.99	Edinburgh (pb)	1-85937-193-0	£8.99
Bournemouth (pb)	1-85937-545-6	£9.99	England In The 1880s	1-85937-331-3	£17.99
Bradford (pb)	1-85937-204-x	£9.99	Essex - Second Selection	1-85937-456-5	£14.99
Bridgend (pb)	1-85937-386-0	£7.99	Essex (pb)	1-85937-270-8	£9.99
Bridgwater (pb)	1-85937-305-4	£9.99	Essex Coast	1-85937-342-9	£14.99
Bridport (pb)	1-85937-327-5	£9.99	Essex Living Memories	1-85937-490-5	£14.99
Brighton (pb)	1-85937-192-2	£8.99	Exeter	1-85937-539-1	£9.99
Bristol (pb)	1-85937-264-3	£9.99	Exmoor (pb)	1-85937-608-8	£9.99
British Life A Century Ago (pb)	1-85937-213-9	£9.99	Falmouth (pb)	1-85937-594-4	£9.99
Buckinghamshire (pb)	1-85937-200-7	£9.99	Folkestone (pb)	1-85937-124-8	£9.99
Camberley (pb)	1-85937-222-8	£9.99	Frome (pb)	1-85937-317-8	£9.99
Cambridge (pb)	1-85937-422-0	£9.99	Glamorgan	1-85937-488-3	£14.99
Cambridgeshire (pb)	1-85937-420-4	£9.99	Glasgow (pb)	1-85937-190-6	£9.99
Cambridgeshire Villages	1-85937-523-5	£14.99	Glastonbury (pb)	1-85937-338-0	£7.99
Canals And Waterways (pb)	1-85937-291-0	£9.99	Gloucester (pb)	1-85937-232-5	£9.99
Canterbury Cathedral (pb)	1-85937-179-5	£9.99	Gloucestershire (pb)	1-85937-561-8	£9.99
Cardiff (pb)	1-85937-093-4	£9.99	Great Yarmouth (pb)	1-85937-426-3	£9.99
Carmarthenshire (pb)	1-85937-604-5	£9.99	Greater Manchester (pb)	1-85937-266-x	£9.99
Chelmsford (pb)	1-85937-310-0	£9.99	Guildford (pb)	1-85937-410-7	£9.99
Cheltenham (pb)	1-85937-095-0	£9.99	Hampshire (pb)	1-85937-279-1	£9.99
Cheshire (pb)	1-85937-271-6	£9.99	Harrogate (pb)	1-85937-423-9	£9.99
Chester (pb)	1-85937-382-8	£9.99	Hastings and Bexhill (pb)	1-85937-131-0	£9.99
Chesterfield (pb)	1-85937-378-x	£9.99	Heart of Lancashire (pb)	1-85937-197-3	£9.99
Chichester (pb)	1-85937-228-7	£9.99	Helston (pb)	1-85937-214-7	£9.99
Churches of East Cornwall (pb)	1-85937-249-x	£9.99	Hereford (pb)	1-85937-175-2	£9.99
Churches of Hampshire (pb)	1-85937-207-4	£9.99	Herefordshire (pb)	1-85937-567-7	£9.99
Cinque Ports & Two Ancient Towns	1-85937-492-1	£14.99	Herefordshire Living Memories	1-85937-514-6	£14.99
Colchester (pb)	1-85937-188-4	£8.99	Hertfordshire (pb)	1-85937-247-3	£9.99
Cornwall (pb)	1-85937-229-5	£9.99	Horsham (pb)	1-85937-432-8	£9.99
Cornwall Living Memories	1-85937-248-1	£14.99	Humberside (pb)	1-85937-605-3	£9.99
Cotswolds (pb)	1-85937-230-9	£9.99	Hythe, Romney Marsh, Ashford (pb)	1-85937-256-2	£9.99
Cotswolds Living Memories	1-85937-255-4	£14.99	Ipswich (pb)	1-85937-424-7	£9.99
County Durham (pb)	1-85937-398-4	£9.99	Isle of Man (pb)	1-85937-268-6	£9.99
Croydon Living Memories (pb)	1-85937-162-0	£9.99	Isle of Wight (pb)	1-85937-429-8	£9.99
Cumbria (pb)	1-85937-621-5	£9.99	Isle of Wight Living Memories	1-85937-304-6	£14.99
Derby (pb)	1-85937-367-4	£9.99	Kent (pb)	1-85937-189-2	£9.99
Derbyshire (pb)	1-85937-196-5	£9.99	Kent Living Memories(pb)	1-85937-401-8	£9.99
Derbyshire Living Memories	1-85937-330-5	£14.99	Kings Lynn (pb)	1-85937-334-8	£9.99

Available from your local bookshop or from the publisher

Frith Book Co Titles (continued)

Title	ISBN	Price	Title	ISBN	Price
Lake District (pb)	1-85937-275-9	£9.99	Sherborne (pb)	1-85937-301-1	£9.99
Lancashire Living Memories	1-85937-335-6	£14.99	Shrewsbury (pb)	1-85937-325-9	£9.99
Lancaster, Morecambe, Heysham (pb)	1-85937-233-3	£9.99	Shropshire (pb)	1-85937-326-7	£9.99
Leeds (pb)	1-85937-202-3	£9.99	Shropshire Living Memories	1-85937-643-6	£14.99
Leicester (pb)	1-85937-381-x	£9.99	Somerset	1-85937-153-1	£14.99
Leicestershire & Rutland Living Memories	1-85937-500-6	£12.99	South Devon Coast	1-85937-107-8	£14.99
Leicestershire (pb)	1-85937-185-x	£9.99	South Devon Living Memories (pb)	1-85937-609-6	£9.99
Lighthouses	1-85937-257-0	£9.99	South East London (pb)	1-85937-263-5	£9.99
Lincoln (pb)	1-85937-380-1	£9.99	South Somerset	1-85937-318-6	£14.99
Lincolnshire (pb)	1-85937-433-6	£9.99	South Wales	1-85937-519-7	£14.99
Liverpool and Merseyside (pb)	1-85937-234-1	£9.99	Southampton (pb)	1-85937-427-1	£9.99
London (pb)	1-85937-183-3	£9.99	Southend (pb)	1-85937-313-5	£9.99
London Living Memories	1-85937-454-9	£14.99	Southport (pb)	1-85937-425-5	£9.99
Ludlow (pb)	1-85937-176-0	£9.99	St Albans (pb)	1-85937-341-0	£9.99
Luton (pb)	1-85937-235-x	£9.99	St Ives (pb)	1-85937-415-8	£9.99
Maidenhead (pb)	1-85937-339-9	£9.99	Stafford Living Memories (pb)	1-85937-503-0	£9.99
Maidstone (pb)	1-85937-391-7	£9.99	Staffordshire (pb)	1-85937-308-9	£9.99
Manchester (pb)	1-85937-198-1	£9.99	Stourbridge (pb)	1-85937-530-8	£9.99
Marlborough (pb)	1-85937-336-4	£9.99	Stratford upon Avon (pb)	1-85937-388-7	£9.99
Middlesex	1-85937-158-2	£14.99	Suffolk (pb)	1-85937-221-x	£9.99
Monmouthshire	1-85937-532-4	£14.99	Suffolk Coast (pb)	1-85937-610-x	£9.99
New Forest (pb)	1-85937-390-9	£9.99	Surrey (pb)	1-85937-240-6	£9.99
Newark (pb)	1-85937-366-6	£9.99	Surrey Living Memories	1-85937-328-3	£14.99
Newport, Wales (pb)	1-85937-258-9	£9.99	Sussex (pb)	1-85937-184-1	£9.99
Newquay (pb)	1-85937-421-2	£9.99	Sutton (pb)	1-85937-337-2	£9.99
Norfolk (pb)	1-85937-195-7	£9.99	Swansea (pb)	1-85937-167-1	£9.99
Norfolk Broads	1-85937-486-7	£14.99	Taunton (pb)	1-85937-314-3	£9.99
Norfolk Living Memories (pb)	1-85937-402-6	£9.99	Tees Valley & Cleveland (pb)	1-85937-623-1	£9.99
North Buckinghamshire	1-85937-626-6	£14.99	Teignmouth (pb)	1-85937-370-4	£7.99
North Devon Living Memories	1-85937-261-9	£14.99	Thanet (pb)	1-85937-116-7	£9.99
North Hertfordshire	1-85937-547-2	£14.99	Tiverton (pb)	1-85937-178-7	£9.99
North London (pb)	1-85937-403-4	£9.99	Torbay (pb)	1-85937-597-9	£9.99
North Somerset	1-85937-302-x	£14.99	Truro (pb)	1-85937-598-7	£9.99
North Wales (pb)	1-85937-298-8	£9.99	Victorian & Edwardian Dorset	1-85937-254-6	£14.99
North Yorkshire (pb)	1-85937-236-8	£9.99	Victorian & Edwardian Kent (pb)	1-85937-624-X	£9.99
Northamptonshire Living Memories	1-85937-529-4	£14.99	Victorian & Edwardian Maritime Album (pb)	1-85937-622-3	£9.99
Northamptonshire	1-85937-150-7	£14.99	Victorian and Edwardian Sussex (pb)	1-85937-625-8	£9.99
Northumberland Tyne & Wear (pb)	1-85937-281-3	£9.99	Villages of Devon (pb)	1-85937-293-7	£9.99
Northumberland	1-85937-522-7	£14.99	Villages of Kent (pb)	1-85937-294-5	£9.99
Norwich (pb)	1-85937-194-9	£8.99	Villages of Sussex (pb)	1-85937-295-3	£9.99
Nottingham (pb)	1-85937-324-0	£9.99	Warrington (pb)	1-85937-507-3	£9.99
Nottinghamshire (pb)	1-85937-187-6	£9.99	Warwick (pb)	1-85937-518-9	£9.99
Oxford (pb)	1-85937-411-5	£9.99	Warwickshire (pb)	1-85937-203-1	£9.99
Oxfordshire (pb)	1-85937-430-1	£9.99	Welsh Castles (pb)	1-85937-322-4	£9.99
Oxfordshire Living Memories	1-85937-525-1	£14.99	West Midlands (pb)	1-85937-289-9	£9.99
Paignton (pb)	1-85937-374-7	£7.99	West Sussex (pb)	1-85937-607-x	£9.99
Peak District (pb)	1-85937-280-5	£9.99	West Yorkshire (pb)	1-85937-201-5	£9.99
Pembrokeshire	1-85937-262-7	£14.99	Weston Super Mare (pb)	1-85937-306-2	£9.99
Penzance (pb)	1-85937-595-2	£9.99	Weymouth (pb)	1-85937-209-0	£9.99
Peterborough (pb)	1-85937-219-8	£9.99	Wiltshire (pb)	1-85937-277-5	£9.99
Picturesque Harbours	1-85937-208-2	£14.99	Wiltshire Churches (pb)	1-85937-171-x	£9.99
Piers	1-85937-237-6	£17.99	Wiltshire Living Memories (pb)	1-85937-396-8	£9.99
Plymouth (pb)	1-85937-389-5	£9.99	Winchester (pb)	1-85937-428-x	£9.99
Poole & Sandbanks (pb)	1-85937-251-1	£9.99	Windsor (pb)	1-85937-333-x	£9.99
Preston (pb)	1-85937-212-0	£9.99	Wokingham & Bracknell (pb)	1-85937-329-1	£9.99
Reading (pb)	1-85937-238-4	£9.99	Woodbridge (pb)	1-85937-498-0	£9.99
Redhill to Reigate (pb)	1-85937-596-0	£9.99	Worcester (pb)	1-85937-165-5	£9.99
Ringwood (pb)	1-85937-384-4	£7.99	Worcestershire Living Memories	1-85937-489-1	£14.99
Romford (pb)	1-85937-319-4	£9.99	Worcestershire	1-85937-152-3	£14.99
Royal Tunbridge Wells (pb)	1-85937-504-9	£9.99	York (pb)	1-85937-199-x	£9.99
Salisbury (pb)	1-85937-239-2	£9.99	Yorkshire (pb)	1-85937-186-8	£9.99
Scarborough (pb)	1-85937-379-8	£9.99	Yorkshire Coastal Memories	1-85937-506-5	£14.99
Sevenoaks and Tonbridge (pb)	1-85937-392-5	£9.99	Yorkshire Dales	1-85937-502-2	£14.99
Sheffield & South Yorks (pb)	1-85937-267-8	£9.99	Yorkshire Living Memories (pb)	1-85937-397-6	£9.99

See Frith books on the internet at www.francisfrith.co.uk

FRITH PRODUCTS & SERVICES

Francis Frith would doubtless be pleased to know that the pioneering publishing venture he started in 1860 still continues today. Over a hundred and forty years later, The Francis Frith Collection continues in the same innovative tradition and is now one of the foremost publishers of vintage photographs in the world. Some of the current activities include:

Interior Decoration

Today Frith's photographs can be seen framed and as giant wall murals in thousands of pubs, restaurants, hotels, banks, retail stores and other public buildings throughout the country. In every case they enhance the unique local atmosphere of the places they depict and provide reminders of gentler days in an increasingly busy and frenetic world.

Product Promotions

Frith products are used by many major companies to promote the sales of their own products or to reinforce their own history and heritage. Frith promotions have been used by Hovis bread, Courage beers, Scots Porage Oats, Colman's mustard, Cadbury's foods, Mellow Birds coffee, Dunhill pipe tobacco, Guinness, and Bulmer's Cider.

Genealogy and Family History

As the interest in family history and roots grows world-wide, more and more people are turning to Frith's photographs of Great Britain for images of the towns, villages and streets where their ancestors lived; and, of course, photographs of the churches and chapels where their ancestors were christened, married and buried are an essential part of every genealogy tree and family album.

Frith Products

All Frith photographs are available Framed or just as Mounted Prints and Posters (size 23 x 16 inches). These may be ordered from the address below. From time to time other products - Address Books, Calendars, Table Mats, etc - are available.

The Internet

Already fifty thousand Frith photographs can be viewed and purchased on the internet through the Frith websites and a myriad of partner sites.

For more detailed information on Frith companies and products, look at these sites:

www.francisfrith.co.uk
www.francisfrith.com
(for North American visitors)

See the complete list of Frith Books at:

www.francisfrith.co.uk

This web site is regularly updated with the latest list of publications from the Frith Book Company. If you wish to buy books relating to another part of the country that your local bookshop does not stock, you may purchase on-line.

For further information, trade, or author enquiries please contact us at the address below:
The Francis Frith Collection, Frith's Barn, Teffont, Salisbury, Wiltshire, England SP3 5QP.
Tel: +44 (0)1722 716 376 Fax: +44 (0)1722 716 881 Email: sales@francisfrith.co.uk

See Frith books on the internet at www.francisfrith.co.uk

FREE MOUNTED PRINT

Mounted Print
Overall size 14 x 11 inches

Fill in and cut out this voucher and return
it with your remittance for £2.25 (to cover postage and handling). Offer valid for delivery to UK addresses only.

Choose any photograph included in this book.
Your SEPIA print will be A4 in size. It will be mounted in a cream mount with a burgundy rule line (overall size 14 x 11 inches).

Order additional Mounted Prints at HALF PRICE (only £7.49 each*)
If you would like to order more Frith prints from this book, possibly as gifts for friends and family, you can buy them at half price (with no additional postage and handling costs).

Have your Mounted Prints framed
For an extra £14.95 per print* you can have your mounted print(s) framed in an elegant polished wood and gilt moulding, overall size 16 x 13 inches (no additional postage and handling required).

---

* IMPORTANT!

These special prices are only available if you order at the same time as you order your free mounted print. You must use the ORIGINAL VOUCHER on this page (no copies permitted). We can only despatch to one address.

Send completed Voucher form to:
The Francis Frith Collection, Frith's Barn, Teffont, Salisbury, Wiltshire SP3 5QP

CHOOSE ANY IMAGE FROM THIS BOOK

Voucher for **FREE** and *Reduced Price Frith Prints*

Please do not photocopy this voucher. Only the original is valid, so please fill it in, cut it out and return it to us with your order.

Picture ref no	Page no	Qty	Mounted @ £7.49	Framed + £14.95	Total Cost
		1	Free of charge*	£	£
			£7.49	£	£
			£7.49	£	£
			£7.49	£	£
			£7.49	£	£
			£7.49	£	£
Please allow 28 days for delivery			* Post & handling (UK)		£2.25
			Total Order Cost		**£**

Title of this book . . . .

I enclose a cheque/postal order for £ . . . .
made payable to 'The Francis Frith Collection'

OR please debit my Mastercard / Visa / Switch / Amex card
(credit cards please on all overseas orders), details below

Card Number

Issue No (Switch only)   Valid from (Amex/Switch)

Expires   Signature

Name Mr/Mrs/Ms . . . .

Address . . . .

. . . .

. . . .

. . . . Postcode . . . .

Daytime Tel No . . . .

Email . . . .

Valid to 31/12/05

Would you like to find out more about Francis Frith?

We have recently recruited some entertaining speakers who are happy to visit local groups, clubs and societies to give an illustrated talk documenting Frith's travels and photographs. If you are a member of such a group and are interested in hosting a presentation, we would love to hear from you.

Our speakers bring with them a small selection of our local town and county books, together with sample prints. They are happy to take orders. A small proportion of the order value is donated to the group who have hosted the presentation. The talks are therefore an excellent way of fundraising for small groups and societies.

Can you help us with information about any of the Frith photographs in this book?

We are gradually compiling an historical record for each of the photographs in the Frith archive. It is always fascinating to find out the names of the people shown in the pictures, as well as insights into the shops, buildings and other features depicted.

If you recognize anyone in the photographs in this book, or if you have information not already included in the author's caption, do let us know. We would love to hear from you, and will try to publish it in future books or articles.

Our production team

Frith books are produced by a small dedicated team at offices in the converted Grade II listed 18th-century barn at Teffont near Salisbury, illustrated above. Most have worked with the Frith Collection for many years. All have in common one quality: they have a passion for the Frith Collection. The team is constantly expanding, but currently includes:

Jason Buck, John Buck, Douglas Mitchell-Burns, Ruth Butler, Heather Crisp, Isobel Hall, Julian Hight, Peter Horne, James Kinnear, Karen Kinnear, Tina Leary, David Marsh, Sue Molloy, Kate Rotondetto, Dean Scource, Eliza Sackett, Terence Sackett, Sandra Sampson, Adrian Sanders, Sandra Sanger, Julia Skinner, Lewis Taylor, Shelley Tolcher and Lorraine Tuck.